BUILDING A
UNIFIED CHURCH

Study by Robert Shippey, Jr.
Commentary by Cecil Sherman

Free downloadable Teaching Guide for this study available at

NextSunday.com/teachingguides

NextSunday Resources
6316 Peake Road
Macon, Georgia 31210-3960
1-800-747-3016
©2019 by NextSunday Resources
All rights reserved.

TABLE OF CONTENTS

Building a Unified Church

HOW TO USE THIS STUDY

NextSunday Resources Adult Bible Studies are designed to help adults study Scripture seriously within the context of the larger Christian tradition and, through that process, find their faith renewed, challenged, and strengthened. We study the Scriptures because we believe they affect our current lives in important ways. Each study contains the following three components:

Study Guide

Each study guide lesson is arranged in four movements:

Reflecting recalls a contemporary story, anecdote, example, or illustration to help us anticipate the session's relevance in our lives.

Remembering provides a frame of reference for the Scriptures.

Studying is centered on giving the biblical material in-depth attention while often surrounding it with helpful insights from theology, ethics, church history, and other areas.

Understanding helps us find relevant connections between our lives and the biblical message.

What About Me? provides brief statements that help unite life issues with the meaning of the biblical text.

Commentary

Each study guide lesson is accompanied by an additional, in-depth commentary on the biblical material. Written by a different author than the study guide, each commentary gives the opportunity for learners to approach the Scripture text from a separate but complementary viewpoint.

Teaching Guide

In addition to the provided study guide and commentary, *NextSunday Resources* also provides a *free* downloadable teaching guide, available at NextSunday.com. Each teaching guide gives the teacher tools for focusing on the content of each study guide lesson through additional commentary and Bible background information. Through teacher helps and teaching options, each teaching guide also provides substance for variety and choice in the preparation of each lesson.

NextSunday
Resources

STUDY INTRODUCTION

Every Christian is a priest, a minister, and a representative of God on earth. Each of us is an extension of the very life and ministry of Christ in a world that deserves to see his love expressed in the gathered community we call church. More than an institution, the church is a living, vibrant organism whose purpose is defined by God as the place where the divine chooses to manifest the work of grace. The church is the place where, in Christ, the love of God is received, shared, and contemplated in both worship and mission.

The sessions in this study reflect on the work of the church in light of the cross, challenging church members to consider how priorities in worship and ministry witness to the wisdom of God, which is Jesus Christ crucified. In his letters to the Corinthians, Paul calls the church to unity of mind and purpose. Yet, perhaps surprising to some, the Apostle's concept of the mind has far less to do with agreement on right doctrine and far more to do with a way of right living in the world. Paul's succinct but profound insight—one that the church has yet to contemplate fully—is this: If God chose to reveal divine love in the cross of the Son, then surely the community gathered in his name would do well to show that same love, both to each other and to the world.

What common purpose unifies the church? What strengthens the church? What weakens the church? What are the building blocks upon which our church is built? These are the central questions for the following study that reflect on our call to build a unified church that is resolute in its understanding of the wisdom of God that humbles the great and lifts up the lowly. We long for the kingdom to come where we are one in Christ Jesus, but in the meantime, we also work in the present to make the kingdom happen through our memory of the cross and its message of redemptive love.

These sessions challenge the church to make the wisdom of God, which is Jesus Christ crucified, a priority in living. The call is to allow the cross to embrace the church so that each of us can understand anew the heart of God and see all that is aflame with Christ's presence in the world. In the process, we are to be both transformed and transforming through the power of divine love.

A CALL FOR UNITY IN MIND AND PURPOSE

1 Corinthians 1:10, 18:31

Central Question

What common purpose unifies the church?

Scripture

1 Corinthians 1:10, 18-31 Now I appeal to you, brothers and sisters, by the name of our Lord Jesus Christ, that all of you be in agreement and that there be no divisions among you, but that you be united in the same mind and the same purpose.... 18 For the message about the cross is foolishness to those who are perishing, but to us who are being saved it is the power of God. 19 For it is written, "I will destroy the wisdom of the wise, and the discernment of the discerning I will thwart." 20 Where is the one who is wise? Where is the scribe? Where is the debater of this age? Has not God made foolish the wisdom of the world? 21 For since, in the wisdom of God, the world did not know God through wisdom, God decided, through the foolishness of our proclamation, to save those who believe. 22 For Jews demand signs and Greeks desire wisdom, 23 but we proclaim Christ crucified, a stumbling block to Jews and foolishness to Gentiles, 24 but to those who are the called, both Jews and Greeks, Christ the power of God and the wisdom of God. 25 For God's foolishness is wiser than human wisdom, and God's weakness is stronger than human strength. 26 Consider your own call, brothers and sisters: not many of you were wise by human standards, not many were powerful, not many were of noble birth. 27 But God chose what is foolish in the world to shame the wise; God chose what is weak in the world to shame the strong; 28 God chose what is low and despised in the world, things that are not, to reduce to nothing things that are, 29 so that no one might boast in the presence of God. 30 He is the source of your life in Christ Jesus, who became for us wisdom from God, and righteousness and sanctification and redemption, 31 in order that, as it is written, "Let the one who boasts, boast in the Lord."

Reflecting

If you were asked to see the church as a great painting, how would the stroke of the artist's brush paint your life, your contribution, and your place in the congregation? The Dutch painter

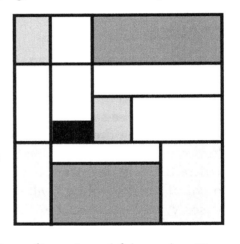

Mondrian was renowned for his ability to paint individual elements on a canvas so that each element maintained its own sense of place over against the whole. For Mondrian, individual lines had meaning in relationship to the whole painting. Similarly, while the church and its members can never be so easily captured in straight lines against the backdrop of a whole painting, the truth is that the church is made up of individuals within community—diversity within unity. Our lives, gifts, journeys, hopes, failures, and joy as people are interwoven. And the church, in some ways, is a recognition of our need for each other.

In a Peanuts© comic strip, Lucy begins, "It's my life." In the second frame she emphatically states, "It's my life and I'll do whatever I want. I'm my own person and I'm the one who has to live it." In the last frame she adds, "With a little help." To the church at Corinth, Paul wrote, "I give thanks to my God always for you." Paul recognized how fortunate he was to be a part of a community of faith and how that community enriched his own life. We are individuals, but God has placed us on a "canvas of living" that connects us to each other. As Martin Luther observed, "It remains, therefore, for us to render mutual service with our gifts, so that each with his own gift, bears the burden and the need of the other" (177).

Remembering

Paul writes this letter to address specific questions the Corinthian church has raised concerning several issues: divisions within the church (vv. 1-4), excessive freedom (vv. 5-7), legitimate versus pagan worship (vv. 8-11), proper understanding of spiritual gifts (vv. 12-14), and questions about the resurrection of the dead (v. 15). Corinth was vital to the Roman Empire as it was an essential port on the major trade route from the west to the orient. This large city was home to a cross-section of people from all over the Roman Empire.

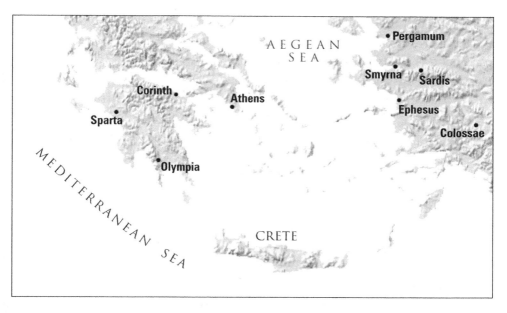

Paul most likely ministered in Corinth around AD 50–51, finding a wealthy city known for its commerce, its temples designed to honor sacred Greek gods, its many social and religious customs, and its reputation for its pagan religious rites and lax morals. We can only imagine the potential problems, but the most pressing problem Paul had to address was the division among the members of the church at Corinth. Some claimed to be disciples of Paul, others of Apollos, Cephas, or Christ. The first four chapters of this letter deal with the problem of division created by emphasizing human leadership and authority at the expense of God's leadership and love.

Studying

In 1:10 Paul strongly advises his fellow believers at Corinth to lead lives marked by the mind and purpose of Christ, not by division. The passage is similar to the letter to the Philippians, which calls believers to testify to the oneness of Spirit and mind, encouraging us to love each other (Phil 1:27-28). Church fellowship cannot happen unless the body is truly of one mind and purpose. But, given the obvious diversity, how is the church to be of "one mind"? Frank Stagg is helpful in noting that "mind" for Paul is best understood as a verb (338). When Paul calls for the church to be of one mind, he means that they should be willing to serve in a way that is characteristic of Christ.

> Only, live your life in a manner worthy of the gospel of Christ, so that, whether I come and see you or am absent and hear about you, I will know that you are standing firm in one spirit, striving side by side with one mind for the faith of the gospel, and are in no way intimidated by your opponents. For them this is evidence of their destruction, but of your salvation. And this is God's doing. (Phil 1:27-28)

If Paul's emphasis on one mind is understood in light of the cross, then we must realize that, for Paul, faith cannot be thought of strictly in terms of our personal beliefs. Being of the same mind does not mean that everyone must hold a similar opinion. Just as there are many different parts to the body, there also are many ways of contributing to the mission of the church. At the cross, there is room for all willing to humble themselves and take their call to serve more seriously than they take themselves, their opinions, and their cultural perspectives. A life of service lived out in light of the cross is what maintains fellowship and creates unity of mind and purpose.

For Christians who focus on the one purpose of the cross, there is a distinct contrast between human wisdom and the wisdom of God. It is ironic, however, that the wisdom and power of the cross that can unify will seem foolish to the world. For Paul, godly wisdom is filled with the positive force of redemption. The wisdom of the cross is the way of salvation and meaningful living.

Giving all of ourselves to God leads to spiritual fulfillment. And just as important, to live accordingly lies in stark contrast to our human tendency to focus on ourselves rather than to give completely and selflessly for the glory of God. Paul states in verse 22, "For Jews demand signs and Greeks desire wisdom." In Paul's understanding, the Jewish quest for a sign and the Greek pursuit of the intellect are one and the same. Looking for signs points to the need for proof, while the desire for human wisdom reflects our need to "master the universe." Both ways point to human achievement as superior. But the truth of the cross tells us that we can't earn our place in God's kingdom and we can't get there on our own. The cross is a gift that cannot be fully understood or received until we are totally dependent on God revealed in Jesus Christ (1:18-25).

Because the cross is an example of the wisdom of God, Paul says that humility, not boastful arrogance, leads to God (1:29). The Corinthians to whom Paul wrote were a living example of God's extraordinary capacity to choose the common and the ordinary to accomplish God's work in the world. Noble birth and powerful position are not the ways of God. Instead, those who are weak and completely dependent, along with those who have a deep sense of something missed apart from Christ, inherit the kingdom (Mt 5:3). God in Christ Jesus is the source of all meaning and life. People who join together and claim their dependency on God are the Christian community—the church. And to be in Christ is a dynamic way of living that allows the community to love unselfishly so that genuine fellowship that glorifies God can be experienced. The church in Christ has a unified purpose of service that positively impacts the world.

Understanding

From time to time, the church has to be reminded to emphasize right living, or *orthopraxis*, over right doctrine, or *orthodoxy*. Likewise, Paul begins his letter to the Corinthians by stressing the need for Christians to live as Christ lived. The spirituality of faithful believers and the integrity of the church are about how we live with, relate to, and serve others.

Yet, even a bold statement such as that does not decrease the need for doctrine or the truth it contains. The point, however, is that what we think about God should be guided by our dependency on God as well as our service to God. We can only imagine how much more effective the church would be in its witness if it were utterly consumed by a desire to "do justice, and to love kindness and to walk humbly with your God" (Mic 6:8). The issue for Paul is authority. But the authority of Christ that Paul emphasizes runs contrary to human logic. Recognizing the weaknesses of human logic starts us on the journey toward God's kind of logic—a journey that requires faith and our belief in the ultimate power of God.

Bishop Desmond Tutu, Nobel peace laureate, observed that sin is fundamentally centrifugal.

Just as a centrifuge uses centrifugal force to push things outward from a center of rotation, so does sin force us outward from the center axis of life. In other words, sin pushes us away from our center in Christ. But Tutu also noted that forgiveness, in contrast to sin, can be considered selfish because being able to forgive leads one to redemption, harmony, and peace with God.

This upside-down kind of logic is the heart of the Christian faith. The unity of the church must be characterized by a will to forgive, embrace, trust, and serve each other. The extent to which we as the church can move beyond our differences to embrace our common unity in Christ directly reflects how close we will come to realizing God's intentions for us. At that point, the church will also become fully the beacon of faith and the source of meaning for a world desperately in need of the One who has come to strengthen through the wisdom of the cross.

What About Me?

• *Who wants to be a "nobody"?* Paul emphasizes that our boasting should be in the Lord. Most of us aspire to be people of influence. Few, if any, of us want to be merely "ordinary." But this is precisely Paul's point. Titles, status, and influence can get in the way of our complete reliance upon God. The call is one of complete trust and faith in the wisdom of God, a wisdom that runs contrary to the wisdom of the world.

• *Is there trouble anywhere?* How does Paul's teaching on various divisions within the church at Corinth speak to modern denominationalism? Paul's emphasis was on God's authority, but the struggle within the Corinthian church was over their loyalty to human authorities. Giving ourselves completely to Jesus Christ means placing that calling above all else. The cross of Christ becomes the guiding symbol that ultimately unifies the church.

• *Do right actions lead to right doctrine, or vice versa?* It is the "Which came first?" question, the chicken or the egg? The church should be characterized by people who love and embrace each other's differences in understanding. But should doctrine set appropriate boundaries for a community of faith?

• *Christians must reject the ways of the world in favor of God's ways.* What does it mean for us to seek justice, mercy, and lovingkindness? How does our church give in to the ways of the world? How does our church succeed in following the ways of God?

Resources

Richard B. Hays, "First Corinthians," *Interpretation: A Bible Commentary for Teaching and Preaching*, ed. Paul J. Achtemeier (Louisville: John Knox Press, 1997).

Martin Luther, *Martin Luther's Basic Theological Writings*, ed. Timothy F. Lull (Minneapolis: Fortress Press, 1989).

Frank Stagg, "Philippians 1:27–2:18: The Mind in Christ Jesus," *Review and Expositor* (Louisville: Southern Baptist Theological Seminary, 1980).

A CALL FOR UNITY
IN MIND AND PURPOSE

1 Corinthians 1:10, 18-31

Introduction

Nearly two thousand years ago, Paul wrote to the Corinthian church, saying, "Now I appeal to you, brothers and sisters, by the name of our Lord Jesus Christ, that all of you be in agreement and that there be no divisions among you, but that you be united in the same mind and the same purpose" (1 Cor 1:10). Although that sentence was written about 1,950 years ago, it could have been written today to Baptists and Presbyterians, Episcopalians and Lutherans. Christ's church is broken into factions called denominations; we hardly talk to each other, much less work together.

The above paragraph was written to include all Protestants. Baptists and Methodists, Catholics and Pentecostals need to think about what our division does to the kingdom of God. When my daughter worked as a missionary-helper in Japan, she was often asked by non-Christians, "Of which Christian sect are you?" This hurts our witness and the reputation of the church.

Our study is "Building a Unified Church." All four sessions come from three chapters in 1 Corinthians. Division in that church is not much different from division in our churches. It doesn't take much imagination to connect Corinthian unity problems with our unity problems. With one eye I'm going to be in the text and working from Corinth. With the other eye I'm going to be looking at our churches today.

We need to remember these things about Corinth:
(1) Corinth was not just any big town. "During Paul's lifetime Corinth ranked with Rome, Alexandria, and Ephesus as the most important cities in the Roman Empire" (Raymond B. Brown,

The Broadman Commentary, Vol. 10, Nashville: Broadman Press, 1970, 287). It was not by accident that Paul stayed in Corinth eighteen months and Ephesus three years. He started churches in the hubs of the empire.

(2) Corinth was commerce. William Barclay said, "A glance at the map of Greece will show that Corinth was made for greatness" (*The Letters to the Corinthians*, Philadelphia: Westminster Press, 1956, 1). Just about anything that moved north or south in Greece had to pass through Corinth. But east-west traffic was where the money was. The city was located on a 10-mile-long and 4-mile-wide isthmus. Ships would avoid a 200-mile journey around the most treacherous narrows in the Mediterranean if they made use of a four-mile track called the "Diolkos" or "haul across." Big ships were unloaded; the goods were hauled across and then reloaded on other ships on the other side. What the Panama Canal became in our time, the "Diolkos" was in the 1st-century Mediterranean world. And Corinth was where it happened. Kenneth Chafin put it well: "The city had developed an unapologetic love of things and a love of pleasure" (*The Communicator's Commentary*, 1, 2 Corinthians, Waco TX: Word Books, 1985,18).

(3) Corinth was diverse. When everybody has the same religion, is of the same generation, and has the same aspirations, then you have a pretty good chance to get "everybody on the same page." But when people are different in every way, getting people together becomes a little bit like making your Rubik's cube line up. It's not easy. Barclay quoted Farrar on Corinth this way: "this mongrel and heterogeneous population of Greek adventurers and Roman bourgeois, with a tainting infusion of Phoenicians; this mass of Jews, ex-soldiers, philosophers, merchants, sailors, freedmen, slaves, trades-people, hucksters." (*The Letters to the Corinthians*, 4). Imagine trying to make a church of that. Unity at Corinth would be hard to attain.

(4) Corinth was immoral. It is true, but not the focus of our studies.

(5) Paul founded the church at Corinth. He came to the city about AD 50, stayed eighteen months and went to Ephesus. From

Ephesus he wrote back to Corinth. Our text should be dated about AD 54 to 55.

(6) The tone of the Corinthian correspondence is friendly but corrective, kind but not approving. It is not like the Galatian letter where he laid rough hands on a wayward people. Here, tenderness persuades. Paul loved these people and it shows.

How Important Is Unity?, 1:10-17.

The Corinthian church had a grocery list of ills. Consider their fellowship diseases:
• 1:10 to 4:21 factions in the church.
• 5:1-13 immorality in the church.
• 6:1-11 lawsuits among members of the church.
• 6:12-20 confusion about proper sexual conduct in the church.
• 7:1-40 confusion about the right way to do marriage in the church.

The list could run on, and Paul knew all these "problems" before he wrote. Which one did he handle first? Unity. Ken Chafin said, "The fact that he puts this problem first and continues the discussion for four chapters indicates that he feels it is of great importance" (*The Communicator's Commentary*, 1, 2 Corinthians, 32).

Paul wanted the Corinthians to function as a church so the gospel could thrive in Corinth and individuals could come to Christian maturity. The goal was unity. "Now I appeal to you, brothers and sisters, by the name of our Lord Jesus Christ, that all of you be in agreement and that there be no divisions among you, but that you be united in the same mind and the same purpose" (1:10). One could conclude that unity is the "highest good" to Paul, and by implication, unity should be the "highest good" to us.

Let me illustrate how treacherous this territory is:
• Did Martin Luther sin when he divided the Roman church, taking the Lutherans? Should he have found a way to stay within?
• In 1985, about 700 were coming to Sunday school in the church I pastored. In 1955–60 there had been 1,300. I put forward an

agenda to attract young adults. About 70 percent of the church was for my agenda and 30 percent were against it. One older lady said to me, "You aren't going to divide our church, are you?" Was keeping everybody happy, together, the "highest good?"

Unity is more important than denominations have made it. We've divided too often, divided over petty stuff, embarrassed the faith, and run off good people. This text speaks to our sin, but unity does not always trump truth, witness or institutional survival.

What Caused Division at Corinth?, 1:12-17.

"For it has been reported to me by Chloe's people that there are quarrels among you....Each of you says, 'I belong to Paul,' or 'I belong to Apollos,' or 'I belong to Cephas,' or 'I belong to Christ.' Has Christ been divided? Was Paul crucified for you?" (1:11-13). The divisions were based on "loyalties to other persons.... The fact that the letter is addressed to the whole church likely indicates that while factions exist, they have not hardened into irreconcilable camps. The believers are not separated from the church but separated within it" (Brown, *The Broadman Commentary*, Vol. 10, 301).

Some Corinthians had been pagan and others Jewish. Most were slaves; a few were of means. Some were a half step from loose living, while others were puritan. Most were new to the faith and no doctrinal base had yet been established.

Our churches are like Corinth. Some members have been here for fifty years and they feel a sense of ownership. The country church I served as interim divided the house between "been heres" and "come heres." Young adults have an agenda for church; they want excellence in child-care and youth programs. Older adults want other things. Congregations divide over contemporary or traditional worship. Do we fund evangelism or ministries? In rural churches family systems often control. A church near Richmond called a young pastor. They directed that he should go out and gather new people. He did. Now the new people threaten the old power group. Old members want the new pastor gone. These are some issues dividing our churches.

Commentators speculate about what the party of Cephas was like as compared to the party of Paul or Apollos, but the biblical text tells us very little. What we do know is that Corinthians and moderns can be loyal to their preacher. It is near impossible to follow some pastors. Some congregations become as attached to the old until the new has no chance. This is tragic. Pastor loyalty is good. Church loyalty is better still.

A church is not a club on a college campus where everyone is of the same age and has the same tight agenda. Churches are "cradle to grave," have different perceptions of gospel priority, try to blend rich and poor, educated and commoner. It's easy to see why churches struggle with unity when you consider what a church is and what it tries to do.

What Great Idea Can Pull Us Together?, 1:18-31.

No doubt Paul had pastoral, godly wisdom. Note how he went about the job of pulling divided people together:
(1) He did not just say, "You people stop bickering." That's the desired end, but it will not get the job done. People have to be led to some other and nobler theme.
(2) He did not target one faction; he even-handedly opposed them all (Chafin, *The Communicator's Commentary*, 1, 2 Cor, 36).
(3) He took himself and his ego out of the quarrel. One faction called themselves the "I belong to Paul" group. Of them Paul asked, "Was Paul crucified for you?" (1:13a).
(4) He posted a central doctrine that was greater than any other. "Jews demand signs and Greeks desire wisdom, but we proclaim Christ crucified, a stumbling block to Jews and foolishness to Gentiles, but to those who are the called, both Jews and Greeks, Christ the power of God and the wisdom of God" (1:22-24).

The church was created by the life, death, and resurrection of Jesus Christ, and the life, death, and resurrection of Jesus Christ sustain the church. The church lives to proclaim the life, death, and resurrection of Jesus Christ. And any other idea, argument, wisdom, faction, fussing group is incidental to the first teaching. Paul did not systematically tear down each group though there is a little of this in 1:18-25; he called all groups to the great doctrine of our faith.

When churches stay to task, churches usually stay together. When churches begin to fragment over the task, then factions come. This idea opens a "can of worms." What is the most important work of a church? Paul said it was "proclaiming Christ crucified" (1:23). All other teachings are derivative from and less than. This does not mean churches do but one thing. It means that churches exist for one great task that overrides all others. Justice issues are important. Service is in the style of Jesus. Teaching is necessary if there be a next generation. But the church is to do everywhere in every place what Paul said was priority in Corinth. If we hold to this idea, we will hold together.

For the sake of Jesus, let's do the work of Jesus together. If we can take hold of a saving message, maybe we can save ourselves from endless bickering and division. God help us!

Notes

Notes

A CALL
TO MATURITY

1 Corinthians 2:1-16

Central Question

What factors strengthen the church?

Scripture

1 Corinthians 2:1-16 When I came to you, brothers and sisters, I did not come proclaiming the mystery of God to you in lofty words or wisdom. 2 For I decided to know nothing among you except Jesus Christ, and him crucified. 3 And I came to you in weakness and in fear and in much trembling. 4 My speech and my proclamation were not with plausible words of wisdom, but with a demonstration of the Spirit and of power, 5 so that your faith might rest not on human wisdom but on the power of God. 6 Yet among the mature we do speak wisdom, though it is not a wisdom of this age or of the rulers of this age, who are doomed to perish. 7 But we speak God's wisdom, secret and hidden, which God decreed before the ages for our glory. 8 None of the rulers of this age understood this; for if they had, they would not have crucified the Lord of glory. 9 But, as it is written, "What no eye has seen, nor ear heard, nor the human heart conceived, what God has prepared for those who love him"— 10 these things God has revealed to us through the Spirit; for the Spirit searches everything, even the depths of God. 11 For what human being knows what is truly human except the human spirit that is within? So also no one comprehends what is truly God's except the Spirit of God. 12 Now we have received not the spirit of the world, but the Spirit that is from God, so that we may understand the gifts bestowed on us by God. 13 And we speak of these things in words not taught by human wisdom but taught by the Spirit, interpreting spiritual things to those who are spiritual. 14 Those who are unspiritual do not receive the gifts of God's Spirit, for they are foolishness to them, and they are unable to understand them because they are spiritually discerned. 15 Those who are spiritual discern all things, and they are themselves subject to no one else's scrutiny. 16 "For who has known the mind of the Lord so as to instruct him?" But we have the mind of Christ.

Reflecting

We live in a world that is constantly changing and increasingly becoming smaller. At no other time in the history of civilization has technology developed at the rate we are experiencing today. But likewise, at no other time have the varied cultures of the world become so intermixed that our values stand in conflict.

Over the past 20 years, studies show "increasing cynicism and disillusionment among American adolescents and youth manifested in a loss of faith in others, in the basic institutions of their society, and in themselves. For example, over a 12 year period beginning in the 1980s the percentage of US high school seniors agreeing with the statement, 'Most people can be trusted' fell by more than half from 35% to 15%" (Bronfenbrenner, 3 Aug 2001).

Unfortunately, the results are often a confused state of understanding about purpose, relevance, and certainty. There is a dizziness about it all, which for many has led to a loss of hope for the future. Andrew Delbanco writes:

> I heard a pediatrician remark that over his thirty years of practice the children he treats become less and less responsive to the standard question, "What do you want to be when you grow up?" In the past he got lots of answers following the formula "I want to be like _____," with the name of a sports hero, or a scientist, or even a politician filling in the blank. Now he gets a shrug, or an I "dunno," or sometimes, the name of a TV cartoon character. Nothing it seems to me is more alarming than our children's incapacity to imagine the future. (98)

In a world where confusion abounds, many are asking, "What is emerging in our midst?" But if faith is anything, it is hope in the future of God's story and how this story provides fulfillment as well as context for living. Such hope in God is necessary if the church is to be strong in its mission. Hope in God's story also calls the church to think about how the gospel can be understood anew, continuing as an example for meaningful living and as a reminder of God's love.

Remembering

To understand the second chapter of Corinthians, you have to recognize that Paul emphasizes the power of the cross as the power of God. Paul acknowledges that God's kind of power won't make sense to the rest of the world, but Christians can understand it. He says that the cross is "foolishness to those who are perishing, but to those who are being saved it is the power of God" (1:18). Individual pride is an offense to the cross, because such pride disregards the power and presence of God. Both human sin and achievement stand judged by this cross, so each of us must recognize complete and total dependency on God for salvation and fulfillment in living. Paul is very clear in suggesting that the wisdom of God is the crucified Christ.

This idea is profound and requires that we stop to consider the depth of God's love. Through Christ's death, God completely absorbs all that is finite and all that is human. Difficult to explain and difficult to understand, the depth of love that the cross conveys means that Christ's death is absorbed into the bosom of God. In doing so, all that is finite and all that limits us, including death, is absorbed into the heart of God as well.

Even in those places where we are most vulnerable and most deeply hurt, in Christ we are not alone because through the cross, his love encircles our living and our dying. The church at Corinth experienced the salvation of the cross and in the place of division and alienation, community was born. In the death of the Son, the strength of salvation is made possible. The church at Corinth found this strength so that the mind and purpose of Christ became their reason for living.

Studying

Fresh from his failure to begin a church in Athens, Paul moved to Corinth. Considering his disappointment for all that had not materialized in Athens, the Apostle had good reason to enter the city of Corinth "in weakness and in fear" and "in much nervousness" (Barclay, 23). From anything but a sense of confidence in himself, Paul preached the cross of Jesus Christ, which he believed to be the essence of the gospel, the Christian faith, and the church. In our text, Paul seems to be suggesting that despite his less than eloquent delivery, the Corinthians believed. This idea encourages the notion that the Holy Spirit was at work using Paul's faithfulness to communicate the secret, or mystery, of God.

Platonic dualism is the belief that our existence has a neat and clean divide between two realms. The first, and most real, is the realm of ideas and spirit. The second, and less real, is the realm of the physical world, the flesh.

The secret, or mystery, of God, however, was unlike anything the Corinthians had ever heard. After all, the culture in which the Corinthians lived was immersed in the tensions between good and evil. Mystery religions emphasized all manner of secret ritual leading followers to believe they were saved if they could somehow discover enlightenment. It is in this context that Paul shares the mystery, or secret, of God. The secret of God is in fact plain for all who have the will or maturity to see. Namely, the power of God is the knowledge of "Jesus Christ, and him crucified" (2:2, 7).

Marion Soards states that "the Corinthians came to believe, not by showy human effort, but by the very working of God's power. Although humans are God's agents, God alone is the one who saves humanity" (1168).

The core of God's story is Jesus Christ—his life, death, and resurrection. To embrace and believe this story is to have our questions, thoughts, answers, dreams, relationships, and pursuits radically changed. Paul understood that Christian maturity was found not in

An expression used by German theologian Dietrich Bonhoeffer, "costly grace," as compared to "cheap grace," is grace which is serious about the need for real repentance and transformation.

human wisdom, but in the wisdom of God that can never be separated from the cross of Christ. Why is it so difficult for people to comprehend that the all-powerful, all-knowing, unchanging will of God is experienced in the depth of love revealed in the cross? Perhaps it is because we are concerned that if this is the way of God, then it may also be the way for those who really believe. Salvation is not a means of escape from the burdens of this world, but a way of life that leaves, even demands, a legacy of service. And the result of that service is eternal relationship with God. Only "costly grace" can make sense of this point. The world cannot even begin to understand it (2:14, 16).

Our text focuses on the need for spiritual discernment in church. Paul believes that only those who are mature in faith and guided by the Spirit achieve such wisdom, which is the mind of Christ. Barclay has observed that the text distinguishes between two kinds of people: the *psuchikos* and the *pneumatikoi*. The *psuchikos* are those who live as if there is nothing beyond our physical lives and the quest for material needs. The *pneumatikoi*, on the other hand, are those who, having received God's wisdom, are sensitive to and guided by the Spirit of God (28). God's wisdom is available, but comes only through living faithfully as a people of true dedication to the cross of Christ (2:10-16).

> Paul declares that God's wisdom is not available to minds that merely inquire. On the contrary, the depths of God's will and work come to humanity only as God chooses to reveal them through the Spirit. Paul states that an unspiritual human is unable to receive the things of the Spirit of God because these things are discernible only by the Spirit (Soards, 1168).

Understanding

The real tragedy in the church is that so many who consider themselves faithful are content to remain at a beginning stage of faith. In expressing the mystery of God, Paul's emphasis is that there are stages in the Christian faith and that the power of God at work in the cross is the believer's call to service. Even now, this call to live out the gospel remains the journey toward spiritual maturity and wisdom.

When the church acknowledges this spiritual journey, it becomes as Christ, called to continue God's divine work in the world. Bill J. Leonard writes, "As Christians live out the gospel, they continue to express the word of God in flesh. As they respond to concrete human need, they continue the incarnate work of Christ. They make His love to be seen in human lives" (27). The ongoing invitation for both individuals and the church is to be caught up in this work of the Spirit so that the church and the world can experience the love and power of God.

In the previous corporate battle between Microsoft and America Online for control of the Internet, an AOL executive remarked of Microsoft, "They're trying to build what we already have" (Buckman and Angwin, B1). Similarly, the world is trying to seek what the church has already been given: wisdom. Long ago, Job questioned what the world is still trying to obtain: "But where shall wisdom be found? And where is the place of under-standing? Mortals do not know the way to it, and it is not found in the land of the living" (Job 28:12-13). The wisdom of God is best understood through the sacrifice of the cross.

As recorded in Acts, "in him we live and move and have our being" (Acts 17:28). Over our failures, emptiness, guilt, desires, and foolishness, Christ is the hope, the light, and the way. He alone can strengthen the church if only the church is willing. The church can remain strong, vibrant, and relevant if it is willing to discern the way of Christ and desires to be the hands and feet of Christ in the world. The great temptation of the church, however, is to dwell on our shortcomings. In doing so, we are prone to judge each other because of our insecurities and inability to control. Almost in spite of ourselves, God's great invitation to the church remains. It is the call to participate in the work of grace where we are able to love as Jesus did because the cross has opened us to the heart of God.

What About Me?

• *The church sings, "Strength for today and glad hope for tomorrow, great is thy faithfulness Lord unto me." But the world is singing, "Is there anybody listening; is there anybody who really cares?" The vast* difference between the two defines our time. The church has the wisdom of God and the hope for the future that the world is so desperately seeking. How can the church bridge the gap? How do we explain how the cross expresses God's love?

• *How do the weaknesses, disappointments, and struggles of our lives strengthen our awareness of God's presence and love?* The extent to which we recognize that we don't have answers to life's most difficult questions is also the extent to which we can be open to God. Why there is pain, suffering, and death in the world is an age-old question. The crucified Christ represents not so much an answer but an orientation for a positive faith in the midst of difficult questions.

• *How does the cross strengthen the church, and how does it open us to the heart of God?* Considering this question allows us to think about what it means to be the people of God in the world. How can the church be of influence in a world desperate for hope and all too aware of judgment?

Resources

William Barclay, *The Letters to the Corinthians* (Philadelphia: The Westminster Press, 1975).

Dietrich Bonhoeffer, *The Cost of Discipleship* (New York: Touchstone, 1995).

Urie Bronfenbrenner, "Growing Chaos in the Lives of Children, Youth, and Families: How Can We Turn It Around?" Parenthood in America proceedings of the conference held in Madison, Wisconsin (19-21 Apr 1998) <http://parenthood.library.wisc.edu/ Bronfenbrenner/Bronfenbrenner.html> (3 Aug 2001).

Rebecca Buckman and Julia Angwin, "Battle to Control Internet Centers on Access, E-Mail," *The Wall Street Journal* (19 June 2001).

Andrew Delbanco, The American Dream: *A Meditation on Hope* (Cambridge: Harvard University Press, 1998).

Richard B. Hays, "First Corinthians," *Interpretation: A Bible Commentary for Teaching and Preaching,* ed. Paul J. Achtemeier (Louisville: John Knox Press, 1997).

Bill J. Leonard, *The Nature of the Church* (Nashville: Broadman Press, 1986).

Marion L. Soards, "First Corinthians," *Mercer Commentary on the Bible*, ed. Watson E. Mills et al. (Macon GA: Mercer University Press, 1995).

E. Frank Tupper, *A Scandalous Providence: The Jesus Story on the Compassion of God* (Macon GA: Mercer University Press, 1995).

A Call
to Maturity

1 Corinthians 2:1-16

Introduction

There is an enormous difference between the early church of Paul and our churches, which lies in the idea of authority. Paul did not write to the Corinthians as I write to you. If you like what I say, you pay attention to it. If you don't, you simply discard it. I have no authority over you; I cannot compel anything of you.

When the church was in its infancy, apostles guided her formation. Paul was one of them. He said of himself, "For I am the least of the apostles, unfit to be called an apostle, because I persecuted the church of God. But by the grace of God I am what I am, and his grace toward me has not been in vain" (1 Cor 15:9-10a). Apostles were given great authority.

I am a church member, but that does not mean I am blind to the weaknesses of our way of "doing church." We give everyone a vote, even those untaught in the Scriptures. Sometimes we place immature people on boards or committees. People who are leaders in the community are often made leaders in the church. This practice seems like a good idea, but usually it isn't.

Strangely, the maturity described in our text does not necessarily pertain to years or education. An individual may have spiritual maturity and have little formal, secular training. Katherine Collins at the Selfs Baptist Church was a devout woman of extraordinary good sense. She did not have a college degree; she had little wealth. For years she taught a Bible class for women, and she became immersed in the things of God. She became wise in a spiritual sense. Our session is speaking of Katherine's kind of wisdom.

This session is about spiritual maturity—about getting to the place where we think like God does (or, put another way, we are thinking God's thoughts). Although the text never says it, the intent of Paul was to pull the Corinthian church together. If they were mature, if they were thinking God's thoughts, then there would not be division. The "party spirit" is not of God. The first four chapters of 1 Corinthians are about "Building a Unified Church." It is not just a study on Christian wisdom; it is wisdom with a point of view to pull a divided people together.

The Message of Paul, 2:1-5.

Is division in the Corinthian church a product of the way the church was born? Did Paul lay the seeds for division when he first preached to them? These five verses seem to be answering these questions.

(1) Paul came with a simple, plain message. "I did not come proclaiming the mystery of God to you in lofty words or wisdom" (2:1a). Paul had lived among the Greeks, so he knew them well. Kenneth Chafin said, "Paul knew that the Corinthians loved big words, clever oratory, and complex logic.... But Paul had decided that this would undermine the message that he brought" (*The Communicator's Commentary*, 1, 2 Corinthians, Waco TX: Word Books, 1985, 44).

If an idea is presented in a needlessly complicated way, that idea is open to several interpretations, but if an idea is put into plain language, then it is not likely to be misunderstood. Paul's method did not create the Corinthian division.

(2) Paul did not ruin the gospel with a high-handed attitude. "I came to you in weakness and in fear and in much trembling" (2:3). An arrogant, haughty speaker can ruin a good idea. People will turn away from truth because of the way it is presented. Paul came with a servant spirit. He did not divide the church because he had an attitude problem.

(3) Paul gave those people entry-level Christianity. "I decided to know nothing among you except Jesus Christ, and him crucified" (2:2). I myself have sinned against this idea. I've had parents bring their children to me. I told them about Jesus, but I told too much. I did not keep it simple, plain. I had to show how smart I

was, and in so doing I confused the child and frustrated the parent. With time I came to Paul's method.

The result of Paul's preaching was a church in Corinth. He got results. "My speech and my proclamation were not with plausible words of wisdom, but with a demonstration of the Spirit and of power" (2:4). Getting results can be a wicked measure for a preacher. It could make any method permissible. But what are we to make of people who preach and get no results? Is that good? Results do matter. The test is to get results and be "in bounds" all at the same time. It's not easy.

The Wisdom of God, 2:6-13.

This passage can make your eyes glaze over and is intimidating to me. "We speak God's wisdom, secret and hidden, which God decreed before the ages for our glory" (2:7). Before diving into the text, let me remind you that the subject is division in the church. Paul is trying to unify the church. He says, "Your division springs from two kinds of wisdom. One group has a wisdom that comes from God. The other group has a wisdom that comes from 'this age.' " Keep this idea in mind as I sort through this text. (1) People who stand especially close to God begin to think God's thoughts. "Yet among the mature we do speak wisdom.... But we speak God's wisdom, secret and hidden" (2:6-7). How do we become "mature"? If we read the Gospels so long that we begin to think like Jesus and we begin to give responses to life situations like Jesus, then we have become like Jesus. Our minds have been transformed and our conduct changed (Rom 12:1-2). That's what Paul means when he speaks of being "mature" as a Christian.

Sometimes people get the idea that this text implies there is a secret club that only an elite few can enter. In fact, that is exactly the opposite of what Paul is saying. The Gnostics were a divisive presence in the early church. They believed that some had special wisdom from God and the rest didn't. Paul worked hard to put those ideas down. They had it wrong.

Anybody can be a "mature" Christian if they will go through the discipleship process. Most church people have come to faith at the "entry level," and that's as far as they've gotten. They could go further, but they choose not to. William Barclay said most Christians come to faith by proclamation of the basic, essential message, "the kerygma." If you want to go further, there is "the didache," which means teachings.

The kerygma is the facts of the faith; the didache explains the meaning of the facts (*The Letters to the Corinthians*, Philadelphia: Westminster Press, 1956, 28-29). Many people can tell you where they walked the aisle, when they were baptized, even who the preacher was, but they haven't a clue what the Bible is about. These people are sometimes quite outspoken in church debates, but they are not mature Christians.

(2) God's wisdom is different from the wisdom of this world. "For what human being knows what is truly human except the human spirit that is within? So also no one comprehends what is truly God's except the Spirit of God" (2:11). Christian history is dotted with people who were worldly but then changed. The Apostle Paul was changed, and he knew the Corinthians could be changed too.

(3) God's wisdom helps us sort out life. "Now we have received the Spirit that is from God, so that we may understand the gifts bestowed on us by God" (2:12). I've seen people with great gifts who could not focus. They had not settled on a purpose or direction. Christian maturity can fix that. I've seen churches with the wrong people in the wrong jobs. Christian maturity can fix that too. Coaches put players in the right places on a team. They fit skills to needs. God's wisdom does the same at church.

The Mind of Christ, 2:14-16.

Paul makes a truthful claim in these verses, which take some explaining. He says, "Those who are spiritual discern all things, and they are themselves subject to no one else's scrutiny" (2:15). Then he goes further to say, "We have the mind of Christ" (2:16b). Obviously, we will need to think carefully about this.

(1) He repeats himself, saying, "Those who are unspiritual do not receive the gifts of God's Spirit, for they are foolishness to them, and they are unable to understand them" (2:14). We've touched on this. "Worldlings" think differently from Christians, and sometimes Christians do things they think are odd, even crazy.

Why do you give a tenth of your money? Why do you worry about sin? They are insensitive to Christian standards. Why do you try to "get involved" in issues of justice and hunger? Of course the answer is that we are working from different presuppositions. Christians who aren't different from "worldlings" aren't very Christian.

(2) "Those who are spiritual discern all things" (2:15a). This text is subject to abuse. Later in this same letter Paul will say, "Now we see in a mirror, dimly, but then we will see face to face. Now I know only in part; then I will know fully, even as I have been fully known" (1 Cor 13:12). At one place he says spiritual people "discern all things," and later he says, "Now I know only in part." What does he mean? Here's my best effort:

• In our text Paul is trying to work through a church fuss. It is not heavy theology; it is personality stuff. We do know how Jesus wants us to love each other. The Gospels are very clear about unity and fellowship issues. See John 13 and 17 for a fuller explanation of what Jesus expects.

• In 1 Cor 13, Paul is sorting through the "tongues" issue. The Gospels give few instructions on that subject. We don't know the mind of Christ on "tongues" nearly so well as we do on fellowship. Some things the Bible does not address fully, and on these subjects we need to make few dogmatic pronouncements.

"Those who are spiritual discern all things" has created havoc in the hands of the wrong preacher-teacher. There is a razor's edge we walk. We are to confidently proclaim the gospel; we are to be humble servant people as we do the gospel. I've had church members who wanted me to tell them things I did not know, and they thought I was less than a preacher for my reservations.

(3) "We have the mind of Christ" (2:16b). I believe this. It is true, I know what Jesus wants me to do most of the time. Once in a while I am confused and can't figure what I ought to do as a Christian. More often, however, my problem is not with "knowing." My problem is with acting right. I believe the church has "the mind of Christ." Our problem is that we don't do what we know.

So knowing the truth is one thing. Telling all of the truth in a decent, caring way is another. You can use truth in a searing, tearing way. Then how do I tell the truth? It is at this point that the "fact of the truth" and the "spirit of the truth-teller" get tangled. "The mind of Christ" is in the untangling. Telling the truth in the spirit of Christ is the target. Sometimes I fall short.

If enough people who care about the church come to spiritual maturity, over a period of time division will go away. And when there is disagreement it will not fester into division. Few issues are worth tearing a church apart . Few issues hurt the reputation of a congregation more than the words, "They are a quarrelsome church." Few themes do more good than those great ideas that pull Christ's people together to common task. Paul was telling those people to grow up in Christ and they would come together in Christ. It's not a bad idea for us.

Notes

Notes

3

WHAT CAUSES DIVISION?

1 Corinthians 3:1-9

Central Question

What contributes to the weakening of the church?

Scripture

1 Corinthians 3:1-9 And so, brothers and sisters, I could not speak to you as spiritual people, but rather as people of the flesh, as infants in Christ. 2 I fed you with milk, not solid food, for you were not ready for solid food. Even now you are still not ready, 3 for you are still of the flesh. For as long as there is jealousy and quarreling among you, are you not of the flesh, and behaving according to human inclinations? 4 For when one says, "I belong to Paul," and another, "I belong to Apollos," are you not merely human? 5 What then is Apollos? What is Paul? Servants through whom you came to believe, as the Lord assigned to each. 6 I planted, Apollos watered, but God gave the growth. 7 So neither the one who plants nor the one who waters is anything, but only God who gives the growth. 8 The one who plants and the one who waters have a common purpose, and each will receive wages according to the labor of each. 9 For we are God's servants, working together; you are God's field, God's building.

Reflecting

In Barbara Kingsolver's tale of life as a missionary in Africa during the early part of the 20th century, Adah, one of the missionary's daughters, reflects:

Cooking meals here requires half the day, and cleaning up the other half. We have to boil our water because it comes from the stream, where parasites multiply in teaming throngs. Africa has parasites so particular and diverse as to occupy every niche of the body.... Outside I saw Mama Tataba, on her way to the kitchen house, dip in a hand and drink straight out of the bucket. I crossed my fingers for her one good eye. I shuddered to think of that dose of God's creation going down, sucking her dry from the inside. (76)

The narrative is poignant because it emphasizes that the very thing so necessary for us to live actually can destroy us from within if we are not careful. In other words, while the issues in life that we anticipate as potential crises seldom happen, those places where we never expected trouble can often be the very places from which difficult struggles surprisingly arise. Likewise, relationships and trust require intentional nurture for community to happen. When we refuse to nurture, the church may find itself unable to move forward because it has allowed fellowship to be diminished from within.

Remembering

Paul believes that only those who are mature in faith and guided by the Spirit receive the true wisdom of God. In the second chapter of our text, the Apostle introduces two kinds of people: those who understand spiritual truth (*pneumatikoi*) and those whose only interests are material need and pleasure (*psuchikos*). The people filled with the Spirit of God have received God's wisdom and have dedicated their lives to contribute toward the ongoing kingdom of Christ. Paul has challenged the Corinthians to be mature in their faith (2:6), but now accuses them of still living at a physical stage instead of having matured (3:1-3).

Studying

Throughout his letters, Paul encourages the church at Corinth to make love its primary aim. He also observes that if the Corinthians had been mature in their faith and resolved to be unified in their love, then they would not be divided. They have instead rallied behind different leaders in a futile effort to gain control. And the result: a church riddled with problems. Had they focused on the true roles of Apollos and Paul, they would have recognized that both were servants with particular gifts. Likewise, they also would have recognized their own responsibility to be servants of God's love (3:5-9).

While the Corinthians perceived themselves to be Spirit-filled, Paul responds directly to their self-centeredness by writing, "I could not speak to you as spiritual people, but rather as people of the flesh, as infants in Christ" (v. 1). Here, he refers to the Corinthian believers as people dominated by the flesh. Because of divisiveness and tensions present within the church, Paul believes that the Corinthians risk their relationship with God. He writes, "For as long as there is jealousy and quarreling among you, are you not of the flesh, and behaving according to human inclinations?" (v. 3). The word translated here as "jealousy" is used by Paul in other places to refer to religious zeal (Phil 3:6, Gal 1:14, Rom 10:2). This notion of religious zeal was fueled by intense debates in the Corinthian church about "proper" understanding and behavior. Richard B. Hays comments,

> When Paul refers to the flesh, his understanding is much larger than a mere preoccupation with material things.

> "As to zeal, a persecutor of the church; as to righteousness under the law, blameless." (Phil 3:6)
> "I advanced in Judaism beyond many among my people of the same age, for I was far more zealous for the traditions of my ancestors." (Gal 1:14)
> "I can testify that they have a zeal for God, but it is not enlightened." (Rom 10:2)

The factions in the community were caused—at least to some extent—by serious questions of theological understanding and religious practice. How do we attain divine wisdom? What actions constitute idolatry? What sexual norms should be observed in marriage? How should manifestations of the Spirit function in worship? What is the meaning of resurrection? These are the sort of issues that were splitting the church, and the different groups were no doubt zealous in their defense of their convictions. (48)

According to Paul, the Corinthian church was far from being focused on the one mind of Christ and the wisdom of God. He says that the priorities that the Corinthian church established were at odds with the Spirit and God's call to serve. The judgment of the Corinthians toward each other only led to God's judgment upon their church. The cross demands more, and their failure to love resulted in their being nothing as the community of God—the church (13:2). What they perceived to be significant was judged as ridiculous in light of the cross. Their lack of love only served to weaken the church from within.

Understanding

Alarming, but true, the extent to which we love our neighbor is actually the extent to which we love God. Regardless of our religious proclamations, offerings, commitments, and activities, if our hearts are filled with pride, prejudice, arrogance, anger, dissension, and judgment, the church and our witness are weakened. Paul preached, "Let your moderation be known to all" (Phil 4:5, 21 KJV). In the name of this or that religious cause, humility and kindness are diminished, and the joy of the Lord's goodness ceases to be felt or realized. When we rally behind this cause or that leader, divisions soon result. Granted, considerable good is sometimes gained by choosing to take a stand for a worthy cause; however, too often we demand what we perceive to be right. By the same token, we so seldom seek God's will that the very cross of Christ becomes diminished for the church, not to mention the world.

Erasmus, a great scholar during the time of the Renaissance observed,

The sum of religion is peace, which can only be when definitions are as few as possible and opinion is left free on many
subjects. (Barzun, 55)

It is difficult for us to think about leaving our definitions of faith
open in order to maintain peace. We think we need standards,
but the standard that has to measure how we conduct ourselves
must be the cross. It is the cross alone that establishes the standard by which the church can practice being the community of
truth. If we are not careful, the quest for righteousness can lead
to a confining religion that burdens us with guilt, which will only
lead to anger and divisiveness.

In William Harris Jr.'s novel *Delirium of the Brave*, a wonderful
story is told about two lifelong friends. Mike is a crusty character
who is a veteran of the Vietnam War. Lloyd, a former professional
football player, has gone to the semi-
nary and become a priest. In reflecting
upon his violent acts in Vietnam, Mike
begins to sob. Lloyd responds by
reminding his friend of the story when

See also
Matthew 8:2-4
and Luke 5:12-14.

Jesus healed the man who had been lowered through a hole in the
roof by his friends. Lloyd recalls that Jesus said to the crippled
man, "Son, your sins are forgiven.... I say to you, stand up, take
your mat and go to your home" (Mk 2:5, 11).

"Do you remember that, Mike?"
Mike finally sat up, wiped his eyes, and said in a detached voice,
"Yeah, I remember."
"Do you remember what happened next?"
"What's the point in all of this, Lloyd? OK, he picked up his
stretcher and walked. End of story."
"No, it's not the end of the story...."
"Don't you see, Michael Sullivan, this guilt that you have
carried around inside of you for so long has crippled you? Let
yourself be forgiven, find the faith you once had, and free your-
self!" (305-306)

Christ is in our midst. If we will be silent and listen, we can
feel his loving presence and be freed. The shackles we have placed
on ourselves burden us with guilt and anger. Rather than dealing

with the deepest burdens of our souls, without even realizing what we are doing, we can judge and condemn others in order to feel better about ourselves. But the game never really works, because we are still refusing to deal with the real problem: our own inadequacies, failures, insecurities, fears, and sins. Within the church, refusal to deal with who we really are and refusal to mend our own hard-hearted spirits can destroy the community from within.

What About Me?

• *The church really is only as vibrant as its individual members.* In what ways can we undergo an attitude adjustment in order to strengthen our church?

• *The lawyer asked Jesus the question, "Who is my neighbor?"* We, too, would do well to reflect on this question, particularly as it relates to our church. Perhaps we have recognized too well the need to love those outside the walls of our church, but have we taken time to embrace those closest to us with whom we worship week after week? What can we do to improve relationships within the church membership?

• *Crossing over the Jordan into the promised land is central to the spiritual journey of the Old Testament.* Not until the people claimed God's vision for their lives were they able to move forward as holy people. Where is the Jordan in our midst? Who is it that God is calling us to be? What is the divine vision for our lives? Will we embrace this vision to genuinely love, care for, and serve each other?

Resources

William Barclay, *The Letters to the Corinthians* (Philadelphia: The Westminster Press, 1975).

Jacques Barzun, From Dawn to Decadence: *500 Years of Western Cultural Life* (New York: Harperperennial Library, 2001).

William Charles Harris Jr., *Delirium of the Brave* (New York: St. Martin's Press, 1998).

Richard B. Hays, "First Corinthians," *Interpretation: A Bible Commentary for Teaching and Preaching,* ed. Paul J. Achtemeier (Louisville: John Knox Press, 1997).

Holy Bible, 21st-Century King James Version (Gary SD: 21st-Century King James Bible Publishers, 1994).

Barbara Kingsolver, *The Poisonwood Bible* (New York: HarperCollins, 1998).

WHAT CAUSES DIVISION?

1 Corinthians 3:1-9

Introduction

Most of the time I've been so deeply immersed in my church that I hardly came up for air. Doing church work is intense, never-ending, and ever-changing. I loved being a pastor, but there were frustrating times when I wondered why I stayed in the job. Usually those hard times came when the church was not unified. Our conflicted ideas of what we ought to do or how we ought to go about it made for tension, sometimes hard feelings, and occasionally business meeting disagreements.

One of the ways I could resolve tension was to drop whatever idea or ministry was causing the problem. But, for me that was often not an option. I would rather be a pastor who was in trouble for doing *something* rather than one who did nothing.

Church divisions are caused by several predictable differences in congregations. They are:

• Generational differences. What young adults demand, senior adults are not ready to provide. What senior adults want, young adults do not make a priority.

• Generational differences over control. It is hard for a seventy-year-old to turn over control to a thirty-five-year-old. How does a church negotiate "passing the baton" of leadership?

• Gospel differences. Some people are concerned about evangelism. Another group wants worship of a certain type to have priority. A third group pushes missions and ministry. And each group has a valid gospel interpretation for their cause.

• The willingness to take church seriously. Some people are ready to give, even sacrifice. Others care for the church...but not that much. The larger group usually controls; the smaller group is a restless presence, and the unevenness tends toward division.

The pastor's job is to get something done without tearing the church apart or getting fired. A pastor is called of God and on mission, but a pastor is also in politics. Pastors are hired by a vote and can be fired by a vote. Most pastors want to hold their churches together; they want to get something done. Those two ideas often work against each other, for churches are notoriously resistant to change.

Paul looked at the Corinthian church and offered his opinions on their division. Let's look at them.

Division Is Caused by Infantile Church Members, 3:1-4.

(1) Our condition. "And so, brothers and sisters, I could not speak to you as spiritual people, but rather as people of the flesh, as infants in Christ." (3:1). The Corinthian problem is our problem. Consider this description of a typical church in America today:
• It is a rare Sunday when half the members are present.
• 80 percent of the money is given by 20 percent of the people.
• Enlisting leaders is often difficult.
• The number of non-resident members is too large.

This is an accurate description of church life in America. Many people identify themselves with church, but the identification is shallow. Why is this the case in so many churches?

For years Kenneth Chafin was a pastor in Houston, Texas. Here is his opinion on why we have so many "babes in Christ" among our members:
• A flawed theology of evangelism will fill a church with immature Christians.
• An anemic understanding of the Bible idea of discipleship; Christian growth is offered as an option rather than a requirement.
• A total preoccupation with numerical growth can fill a church with people; it will not lead those people to spiritual growth

(*The Communicator's Commentary*, 1, 2 Corinthians, Waco TX: Word Books, 1985, 53).

Paul wrote back to Corinth to say, "I fed you with milk, not solid food, for you were not ready for solid food. Even now you are still not ready" (3:2). This means that Paul wanted to tell those people some things, but didn't. They would not have understood him if he had. Talking about serious discipleship is a strange language to "infants in Christ." You might as well speak to them in Greek.

(2) Our sickness. "You are still of the flesh...As long as there is jealousy and quarreling among you, are you not of the flesh, and behaving according to human inclinations?" (3:3). Paul's use of the phrase "of the flesh" needs explanation. We can't keep from being flesh. That's the human condition. But Christians are supposed to rise above our fleshly ways and take on the thoughts and ways of God. We have an idea what that is like by following Jesus' example (Heb 12:2). When Paul said the Corinthians were "of the flesh" he meant "they had not yet got beyond human things.... Corinthians were not only made of flesh but dominated by the flesh.... To Paul the flesh means human nature apart from God"(William Barclay, *The Letters to the Corinthians*, Philadelphia: Westminster Press, 1956, 33).

During the time soon after a person becomes a Christian, it's appropriate to be an "infant in Christ." Nobody begins the Christian life fully grown, but there's sin in staying a baby. At this point the "infants in Christ" idea needs some fine-tuning. If you feed a healthy body, then it will grow. But nurturing the spirit is more like the care and feeding of a baby's *mind*. Not many parents fail to feed their baby, but a lot of parents are careless about what is put into the baby's mind. What do they read? What words are used around the child? What kind of TV is permitted the child? It is this kind of thinking that is getting close to our subject.

Division in the Corinthian church was evidence (and proof) that the people were still "infants in Christ." I've heard doctors say a child asthmatic may "outgrow" his or her asthma. When we grow up in Christ, we grow out of a quarrelsome, contentious spirit. Would that we could outgrow our fussy ways!

Division Is Caused by Misplaced Loyalties, 3:4-7.

"For when one says, 'I belong to Paul,' and another, 'I belong to Apollos,' are you not merely human? What then is Apollos? What is Paul? Servants through whom you learned to believe, as the Lord assigned to each" (3:4-5). When Paul introduced the problem of division in the Corinthian church, he listed four groups: the Paul people, the Apollos party, the Cephas group, and the "I belong to Christ" folks (see 1:12). Assigning specific theological characteristics to these groups is guessing. What we know is that they were subgroups within the church and that they were causing tension.

I can understand this problem. Strong preacher personalities make for strong loyalties. We don't know much about Apollos, but we do know about Cephas (usually called Peter) and Paul. Both were strong leaders, and they did not always agree (Gal 2:1-14). Paul founded the church at Corinth, but Apollos and Peter must have spent time there also. Around each of these leaders grew a party of boosters, and the little booster groups had become a problem to the harmony and function of the church.

When I was thirty-six years old, I became pastor of the Asheville church. I followed Perry Crouch, who had been pastor of the church for twenty years. Dr. Crouch was broadly respected in the community; he had done a very good job with the church. I was stepping into big shoes, and looking back on those days, I realize that I was just a kid.

Soon after my arrival, the church was required to face integration. I had been in the church but six short weeks. Older members of the church remembered the good judgment of Perry Crouch and longed for his sure hand in the difficult decision the church was facing. For a time there was "the Perry Crouch party" in my church. Dr. Crouch did not cause it; he had just served those people well in hard times, and they wanted his services in the present. Time took care of the problem.

But what if time does not make that kind of problem go away? Many churches cling to the memory of the former pastor;

they glorify the accomplishments, and in their nostalgia they paint a picture of the past that makes any present colorless. At this point we are into a cult of personality. The true glory of a pastor is that we are allowed to pastor a good church for a time and then we are gone.

I've stated the ideal, but life is not ideal. When a new pastor takes a church, that pastor cannot mean to the membership what the old pastor does. And what if right at this moment a loved one dies. Do you want one who hardly knows the deceased to do the funeral? Or do you want the old friend, the former pastor? I know how you feel. There is no easy answer to this one, but this text reminds us of the limits in loyalty to a person. It can become destructive to congregational unity.

Division Is Caused by Forgetting Our Interdependence, 3:8-9.

"The one who plants and the one who waters have a common purpose, and each will receive wages according to the labor of each. For we are God's servants, working together; you are God's field, God's building" (3:8-9). Doing church work is different from working in a family business. Imagine that ministers all the way back to the founding of the church are team members. Ministers are working together to enlarge the kingdom of God, and the health of individual churches is one small part of this larger goal. If that is the case, then all ministers are working together in a larger task, and the task consumes individual personality. "The one who plants and the one who waters have a common purpose." I could not have done what I did had it not been for those who went before. Those who come after me are in the same debt. In God's timetable we are here for a short time. A minister's glory is not in a small group that works to perpetuate our reputation. A minister's glory is lost in a larger task.

Holding on to life and reputation is ego-driven and unbecoming to a Christian leader. When the time came for Jesus to go to the cross, he said, "The hour has come for the Son of Man to be glorified.... Unless a grain of wheat falls into the earth and dies, it remains just a single grain; but if it dies, it bears much fruit. Those who love their life lose it; and those who hate their life in this world will keep it for eternal life" (Jn 12:23-25). Reputation, legacy, how history will view us...these are not concerns for mature disciples. "We are God's servants, working together" (3:9a).

Paul knew where he fit in God's scheme of things. We need to rise to the stature of Paul. We need to get our own identity straight. At our best we are God's helpers...that's all.

Notes

Notes

BUILDING ON
A SOLID FOUNDATION

1 Corinthians 3:10-23

Central Question

What are the building blocks upon which the church is built?

Scripture

1 Corinthians 3:10-23 According to the grace of God given to me, like a skilled master builder I laid a foundation, and someone else is building on it. Each builder must choose with care how to build on it. 11 For no one can lay any foundation other than the one that has been laid; that foundation is Jesus Christ. 12 Now if anyone builds on the foundation with gold, silver, precious stones, wood, hay, straw— 13 the work of each builder will become visible, for the Day will disclose it, because it will be revealed with fire, and the fire will test what sort of work each has done. 14 If what has been built on the foundation survives, the builder will receive a reward. 15 If the work is burned up, the builder will suffer loss; the builder will be saved, but only as through fire. 16 Do you not know that you are God's temple and that God's Spirit dwells in you? 17 If anyone destroys God's temple, God will destroy that person. For God's temple is holy, and you are that temple. 18 Do not deceive yourselves. If you think that you are wise in this age, you should become fools so that you may become wise. 19 For the wisdom of this world is foolishness with God. For it is written, "He catches the wise in their craftiness," 20 and again, "The Lord knows the thoughts of the wise, that they are futile." 21 So let no one boast about human leaders. For all things are yours, 22 whether Paul or Apollos or Cephas or the world or life or death or the present or the future—all belong to you, 23 and you belong to Christ, and Christ belongs to God.

Reflecting

Most people who travel to England marvel at the majestic cathedrals like Westminster Abbey, St. Paul's, and St. George's, all great buildings arrayed in splendor. In looking at the beauty of these cathedrals and the marvel of their construction, one can stand amazed realizing that they were built centuries ago, one stone at a time. Who were the unknown stone masons and makers of glass who carved into creation

the beauty that we now behold? More poignantly, what stones are we currently laying that contribute, even in the smallest of ways, to the beauty of our church and the world?

Ben Campbell Johnson and Glenn McDonald describe the church as "a living community of faith composed of living stones that draw their life from the foundation stone" (13). The great opportunity for the church in every age is to be a living community that gives life to the world by radiating with the love of Jesus Christ. Paul speaks of a vision in which the church that is in Christ belongs to God. As such, the church is God's project. God is in control, but the church is invited to participate in a future that has exciting possibilities whose end only God knows.

Remembering

Central to Paul's understanding of the church is the depth of God's love revealed in the cross of Jesus Christ. The Apostle's profound awareness of God's endless capacity to love sacrificially shapes how he thinks the church should minister in the world.

He also recognizes absolute dependency on Jesus Christ as the way of redemption and maintains that all achievement and insight should be attributed to Christ. In other words, all that we are, become, accomplish, and aspire to do is an effect of the redemptive work of God.

When Paul writes, "Let the one who boasts, boast in the Lord" (1:31), he's highlighting the point that church members belong to Christ, just as Christ belongs to God (3:23). Belonging to Christ transforms our lives. In Paul's view, that transformation allows the church to be a place where "there is no longer Jew or Greek, there is no longer slave or free, there is no longer male and female, for all of you are one in Christ Jesus" (Gal 3:28). In fact, Paul's letter to the Corinthians challenges the church to put aside issues that pale in significance to the cross so that all its members can participate in a holy community absent of pride, short-sightedness, and divisiveness. All that we are, as a people of faith, stems from the grace of God working in us.

Studying

Paul introduces the metaphor of architecture to emphasize the importance of the building blocks necessary for building the church. Interestingly, while imagery of a building might cause readers to think of a structure that does not change, Paul's concept of church is active—a living, growing body. Central to his understanding are the opening words of Psalm 127: "Unless the Lord builds the house, those who build it labor in vain." Verse 9 describes the Corinthians as a building where Paul has laid the foundation. Now Apollos and other servants are being entrusted to build the structure. Having already railed against human wisdom, Paul insists that the true foundation is Jesus Christ. If Jesus Christ is the foundation, then the work of the church is an ongoing extension of Jesus' ministry on earth. While the gist of Jesus' teachings cannot be simply packaged, his call to "love the Lord your God with all your heart and with all your soul and with all your mind and with all your strength," along with his advice to "love your neighbor as yourself," summarizes the work of the church (Mk 12:30-31).

Verse 12 further develops the metaphor of the building by calling attention to the quality of the materials used in its construction. The pending day of judgment will reveal the attitudes of those who have participated in the building process. The meaning of the various elements is difficult to determine. One possible explanation is that the more gifted will use gold, silver, and precious stones. Those less fortunate may use wood, hay, or straw. Despite the kind of material used, however, in God's time, the attitude of each builder will be revealed. Another possibility might be that the first elements are fireproof and will stand the test of time. And since fire produces radiant light, Paul may have in mind a use of materials that will allow the church to be a light unto the world. Such materials are long-lasting, especially when compared with the other elements, which are short-lived and have no substance (vv. 12-13).

Paul means to admonish the Corinthians to a careful selection of materials—that is, to a way of life as a church that is fitting for the foundation of Jesus Christ. Christian works may not bring salvation—after all, God accomplished that in the cross of Christ—but what Christians do with their lives does make a difference in God's eyes (Soards, 1169).

While judgment may be an uncomfortable notion, Paul's imagery of fire clearly indicates that individuals will be held accountable for how they have constructed the church (vv. 14-15). Paul most likely has in mind his belief that the end-time judgment was near (see Rom 2:5; 1 Cor 1:8; and Phil 1:6, 10). But, the passage also reminds us that we need to be aware that our attitudes, thoughts, and service either contribute to or diminish the church.

Verse 16 introduces a final part of the building metaphor, under-scoring how and why the church is understood as God's temple. The integrity of the church is at issue. In a sincere effort, many have confused the notion of entertainment with that of worship, so much, in fact, that they are preoccupied with how church makes them feel. Others are content just to show up and have no desire to reflect or think for themselves. They are satisfied just to be told what to do. Churches can also become so driven by their programs that they lose sight of the ongoing need to discover their particular mission. But true church ought to be a place where questions about God's intimate will and purpose for our lives are welcomed. Worship ought to call out a desire to know God's will, call, and blessing for our lives. Crucial life-questions should be pursued: What is our purpose? What is it that God wants us to do? How can our church contribute to the fulfillment of humankind's greatest spiritual need, which is the transformation of people into children of God called to serve the world?

It is especially important to understand that the Greek word for "you" in verses 16 and 17 is plural. The Spirit dwells in the individual and also in the gathered community. This indwelling of the Spirit is essential if the church is to continue. The wisdom of God that Paul addresses in chapter 1, which is the crucified Christ, cannot be received unless the church, through the indwelling of the Spirit, is unified in mind and purpose to continue Christ's work in the world.

One of the desperate needs of the church is to recapture this vision of what it is by grace, and therefore also what God intends it to be. In most Protestant circles, one tends to take the local parish altogether too lightly. Seldom does one sense that it is, or even can be, experienced as a community that is so powerfully indwelt by the Spirit that it functions as a genuine alternative to the pagan world in which it is found. It is perhaps not too strong to suggest that the recapturing of this vision of its being, both in terms of its being powerfully indwelt by the Spirit and of its thereby serving as a genuine alternative to the world, is its single greatest need (Fee, 149-50).

From a Jewish perspective, the temple was the place where God dwelled and was the indication of God's presence on earth. Remarkably (for the temple in Jerusalem was still in existence at the time of Paul's writing), Paul observes that the place where God's Spirit now dwells is in the Christian church characterized by God's wisdom. So, those who build with shoddy materials or those who undermine the unity of the Spirit need to be aware that they are toying with the very place where God has chosen to be present and the very means by which God works in the world.

Understanding

Robert Nash recounts an experience from his youth when his cross-country coach came up alongside him during a race and called out, "Nash, you're slowing down. What's wrong?" Nash huffed, "Don't worry, Coach! I'll make it to the finish line." The coach shouted back, "Making it to the finish line is not the point! The point is to get better every time you run" (107). Regrettably, many churchgoers are content just to get by. In such cases, commitment to excellence in every facet of the church's life is of no concern or value. A willingness to accept mediocre worship prevails, and the church unwittingly silences its voice to a world that deserves and needs to see the living witness of Jesus Christ.

Small things matter. In his diary of travels abroad, Mark Twain reflects on the ruins of an ancient palace and wonders how even an earthquake could affect such a mass of masonry:

> But we found the destroyer, after a while, and then our wonder was increased tenfold. Seeds had fallen in crevices in the vast walls; the seeds had sprouted; the tender, insignificant sprouts had hardened; they grew larger and larger, and by a steady, imperceptible pressure forced the great stones apart, and now are bringing sure destruction upon a giant work that has even mocked the earthquakes to scorn! (272)

If we are to build the church in dynamic ways that can captivate the world with a worthy vision, then our commitment to worship that leads to service and our willingness to take up the cross and follow Christ really do matter. Our genuine desire to love and embrace each other is imperative. Our need to repent and our desire to live with hearts overcome with grace is essential. Our call to avoid ignorance, to mature, and to

seek excellence and integrity is bedrock. Living by the fruit of the Spirit, which is "love, joy, peace, patience, kindness, generosity, faithfulness, gentleness, and self control" (Gal 5:22), is fundamental. Like the small seeds that took root and eventually brought about the palace's destruction from within, so, too, will our petty judgments, poor attitudes, arrogance, and self-righteousness lessen the light of the church. If we do not live in genuine humility—seeking not only to be transformed by God, but also transforming through the power of God's love—then the light of the church will fade.

What About Me?

• *Can the church be considered a living community of faith composed of living stones?* If so, what stones do we need to contribute and what stones do we need to put aside in order to build the church successfully? How do you interpret Paul's use of gold, silver, precious stones, wood, hay, and straw as elements used to build the church?

• *Why is it important to the church for "all to be one in Christ"?* How can our church achieve that kind of unity? What can be accomplished if the church is not unified?

• *How can the church respond to the crucial questions of life?* Such questions drive at the heart of who we are both as individuals and as the church. What is our purpose? What is it that God wants us to do? How can your church help transform people into children of God called to serve the world?

• *How is the church the visible presence of God's Spirit?* How can the church discern and live out its mission as opposed to managing its programs? How are new people included? What do you think about the vision of your local church, and what would you like that vision to be?

Resources

Gordon D. Fee, *The First Epistle to the Corinthians* (Grand Rapids: Wm. B. Eerdmans, 1987).

Richard B. Hays, "First Corinthians," *Interpretation: A Bible Commentary for Teaching and Preaching*, ed. Paul J. Achtemeier (Louisville: John Knox Press, 1997).

Ben Campbell Johnson and Glenn McDonald, *Imagining a Church in the Spirit: A Task for Mainline Congregations* (Grand Rapids: William B. Eerdmans Publishing Co., 1999).

Robert N. Nash Jr., *An 8-Track Church in a CD World: The Modern Church in the Postmodern World* (Macon GA: Smyth & Helwys Publishing, Inc., 1997).

Marion L. Soards, "First Corinthians," *Mercer Commentary on the Bible*, ed. Watson E. Mills et al. (Macon GA: Mercer University Press, 1995).

Mark Twain, *The Unabridged Mark Twain*, ed. Lawrence Teacher (Philadelphia: Running Press, 1976).

BUILDING ON
A SOLID FOUNDATION
1 Corinthians 3:10-23

Introduction

The Apostle Paul was at the beginning of a work that continues until this day. At first there were only a few, but with time there evolved a small army of people who travel about starting churches or strengthening churches. We call these people missionaries. Usually these people work in places where Christian churches are scarce. They really are successors to Paul; they are church-starters and missionaries.

By what ground rules do missionaries work? The Corinthian church was divided. One reason for the division was the loyalty to missionary preachers who had passed through. " 'I belong to Paul,' or 'I belong to Apollos,' or 'I belong to Cephas,' or 'I belong to Christ' " (1:12) was a part of the Corinthian problem. In American churches there is a slightly different problem; each pastor creates a body of loyal followers. This lesson's text is instruction for pastors or missionaries. Rarely does a man or woman start a church and stay with it as long as the church lasts. The work of the starter is handed over to another. How are these temporary pastors or missionaries to see their work? How are they to make their work interface with other pastors and missionaries? Put another way, are the passing church leaders going to be "team players," or are they going to be soloists?

Two problems:

• Some pastors and missionaries want to be remembered. They labor to create a legacy that will perpetuate their name.

• Some laypeople want a "super-pastor." When you get this kind of following, you have a successor problem.

This text gets at the vanity problem of a pastor-missionary, and it speaks to the tendency of laypeople to exalt church leaders.

Our Work is Building, 3:10-11.

"According to the grace of God given to me, like a skilled master builder I laid a foundation, and someone else is building on it. Each builder must choose with care how to build on it. For no one can lay any foundation other than the one that has been laid; that foundation is Jesus Christ" (3:10-11). Three ideas jump off the page:

(1) "I laid a foundation, and someone else is building on it" (3:10a). Paul didn't start the church at Corinth by himself; others entered into the work to finish what he began. A good leader adds to what another has begun, leaving a church better than he or she found it.

(2) "Each builder must choose with care how to build on it" (3:10b). Pastors and missionaries are accountable for what happens on "their watch."

(3) From the beginning, the stackpole of the church is Christ. Pastors and missionaries are helpers. The "cult of personality" in church work is a sin. It has no place. This means pastors and missionaries are expendable; we are spent to enlarge the church.

Our Test Is Endurance, 3:12-15.

"Now if anyone builds on the foundation with gold, silver, precious stones, wood, hay, straw" (3:12). The bedrock foundation of a good church is Jesus Christ. That foundation will support any ministry, mission, or church. What we stack on top of that foundation is our life work, our stewardship. Paul's illustration here is from the building trade. Buying a house is big; it is the biggest purchase Dot and I have ever made. Before buying, we asked questions about our builder. Did that builder have a good reputation? How long had the builder been in business? I am not in the building business, and I am vulnerable. I've been to Home Depot enough to know that there are all kinds of products. Some are very good, some are pretty good, and some are almost temporary.

Church work can be that way too. There are things a preacher can do that will "make a quick showing." Dramatic and showy preaching will draw a crowd. However, "quick fixes" do little for the church in the long run. I call that kind of stuff building with "wood, hay, straw." The "wood, hay, straw" covers over the foundation that is Jesus Christ. It's not Christ; it's the show that brought and holds them.

There is no hiding shoddy building materials; time will expose the cheap and confirm the good stuff. And church work is like building a house. Paul said, "The work of each builder will become visible, for the Day will disclose it, because it will be revealed with fire, and the fire will test what sort of work each has done" (3:13). "The Day" is Judgment Day and the Judge is God. This means though I may "fool" a congregation into believing I've done good work, there is a Building Inspector waiting who is not subject to any kind of deception.

Clarence T. Craig made a powerful statement in his commentary on 1 Corinthians: "Salvation by grace does not exclude belief in a judgment, even on believers (2 Cor. 5:10; Rom. 3:6)" (*The Interpreter's Bible*, Vol. 10, New York: Abingdon Press, 1953, 48). Paul said, "If the work is burned up, the builder will suffer loss; the builder will be saved, but only as through fire" (3:15).

Our Church Is a Temple, 3:16-17.

"Do you not know that you are God's temple and that God's Spirit dwells in you?" (3:16). I doubt many Protestants think of their church as "God's temple and that God's Spirit dwells in you." (The "you" is plural and refers to the people who make up the Corinthian church.) We are more functional. The church is a building that sits on the corner of First and Commerce. The church is the people who gather on Sunday morning. There is some truth in our functional definitions, but there is a truth that rises above function. That truth elevates the church. It separates our churches from our social clubs.

As a child I remember going into "big church" with my mother and daddy. Everyone was talking in a relaxed sort of way. The conversation was just neighbor talking to neighbor. Then the choir would enter and silence the chatter by singing:

The Lord is in his Holy Temple,
The Lord is in his Holy Temple
Let all the earth keep silence,
Let all the earth keep silence,
Keep silence...before Him.
(George F. Root, *The Baptist Hymnal*, Nashville: Broadman Press, 1926, No. 411)

The purpose of "the call to worship" was to lift our sights. We were not just a casual company of people gathered off the street in Fort Worth. We were "the very temple of God because the Church was the society in which the Spirit of God dwelt" (William Barclay, *The Letters to the Corinthians*, Philadelphia: Westminster Press, 1956, 38). In short order these ideas rise from the text:
(1) Church is serious business and ought to be treated as such. Reverence and awe are attached to the place, worship, and company. "God's temple is holy" (3:17b).
(2) Splitting a church offends God. "If anyone destroys God's temple, God will destroy that person" (3:17a).
(3) God's Spirit makes a home in our churches, and when our churches are divided we make them uninhabitable for God's Spirit. The people who create and stir dissension in a church are not of God's Spirit, nor do they work to the health of any church.

Many churches go out of their way to make a place for everyone. Sometimes this practice opens the door for trouble-makers. Paul says such people are more destructive than we know. I've known some churches that were literally destroyed by the persistent efforts of divisive people. Paul would not have been gentle with divisive people. He would not allow anyone to sap the church of the Spirit of God. They make mockery of Christ's command that we love one another. They discourage the saints.

Our Threat Is "This Age" Wisdom, 3:18-20.

"Do not deceive yourselves. If you think that you are wise in this age, you should become fools so that you may become wise. For the wisdom of this world is foolishness with God" (3:18-19a).

Paul is circling back with his argument. Already, he discussed the trouble that could come to a church by giving place to those who are "wise in this age" (1:18-31). Now he returns to this idea. I think this is a clue for us. The real problem in the Corinthian church was a small group of smug, smart folks who thought they were superior to the rest. Barclay said, "Paul then goes on once again to pin down the root cause of this dissension.... That root cause is the worship of intellectual, worldly wisdom" (*The Letters to the Corinthians*, 38). The smug, smart folks were fussy and exclusive. They "looked down" on the ordinary lot, and the ordinary lot resented the smug, smart folks.

Paul came down on the side of the common lot. He pointed to the cross and Christ crucified as the central, unifying message of the church. He called the church to rally around one great idea; he quoted Job 5:13 and Ps 94:11 to make his point. What Paul did with the fussy Corinthians may be a signal for us. When we explain what we believe, we often get into detail. We want to get it right. That's well and good, but we can call on people to believe too much. Paul didn't get into the implied teachings of believing in Christ. To pull a church together he emphasized one idea.

There's a clue here for us if we are bright enough to catch it.

Our Centerpiece Is Christ, 3:21-23.

"So let no one boast about human leaders. For all things are yours, whether Paul or Apollos or Cephas or the world or life or death or the present or the future—all belong to you, and you belong to Christ, and Christ belongs to God" (3:21-23). The key phrase is, "You belong to Christ." The wisdom of "this age" will change. Paul, Apollos, and Cephas will all die and be gone. The one great theme of the church is Christ! "I decided to know nothing among you except Jesus Christ, and him crucified" (2:2). There are lesser teachings, and they have a place. But they are less than. Emphasize small doctrine long enough and a church will become unbalanced. Emphasize Christ, and a church can right herself and regain perspective.

When Christians look at God, they look through the words and ways of Jesus Christ. In response to Philip's question, Jesus said, "Whoever has seen me has seen the Father" (Jn 14:9b). And looking at God through the lens that is Jesus Christ gives a different picture from looking at God through the words and ways of Moses or Mohammed. This is the difference in being Jewish, Muslim, and Christian. When we are at our best, we are "Jesus people."

There is much to divert us from our central message. On the right are people who want us to emphasize the Bible or prophecy. On the left is a shopping list of ethical issues in some way connected to following Jesus. Both distract us from our task. In a crisis there may be a time when a pastor needs to turn aside and address issues like race or war, the environment or hunger, or correct doctrine. Situations can make this appropriate. But the church of Jesus Christ was called into being by a message about Jesus. It will stay healthy when we stay on message. We are builders; Jesus is the foundation.

Notes

Notes

Made in the USA
Middletown, DE
29 March 2022

63370134R00040